Streets as Elsewhere

Norman, Oklahoma
2014

FIRST EDITION, August 13, 2014

Streets as Elsewhere
© 2014 by J.L. Jacobs

ISBN 978-0-9851337-7-1

Except for fair use in reviews and/or scholarly considerations, no part of this book may be reproduced, performed, recorded, or otherwise transmitted without the written consent of the author and the permission of the publisher.

Cover Image, Portrait:
*Grandmother Charlotte
as Photographed by Grandmother Lottie Marie*

Cover image map by Jimm Jacobs, published in *Traveling Timber Towns* by Fayrene Benson, Bob Burke, Jimm Jacobs (Commonwealth Press, 2004.)

Also by J.L. Jacobs:
Varieties of Inflorescence, LEAVE, 1992
The Leaves in Her Shoes, Lost Roads, 1999
Dream Songs, Above Ground Press, 2004

Mongrel Empire Press
Norman, OK

Online catalogue: www.mongrelempire.org

Book Design: Mongrel Empire Press using iWork Pages

*Charlotte Honeywell Fuller
and for my parents
with love*

The author would like to acknowledge the following publications in which some of these poems first appeared:

First Intensity: "Call it sky," Making of real and unreal," "Of wash rooms," "Slow after moonset," "Streets as Elsewhere"

First Intensity: "A theology of soil," "Closed Rooms," "Grinding into Wood," "All directions of an open field"

Impercipient: "Erasures," "The Look of a River," "August and Rain"

Maple Tree Literary Supplement: "Skirt Hill"

No: A Journal of the Arts: "Under Pretext of Music," "The arsenic furnace," "By Late Morning," "Indian Head Appliqué"

Ploughshares: "Certitude," "Down this wall of heat," "Ramparts of Sound," "Disorders of skin"

Snow*Vigate: "Ultima Thule 1945," "Do we breathe as rain," "Tract of level country," "May without rain," "North to their wives and dying hymns"

Stanzas #39: "A Grace o' Sundays" (seven poem chapter) published in chapbook *Dream Songs*

Streets as Elsewhere was a 2009 Finalist, Green Rose Prize, Western Michigan University Press, and a 2011 Semi-Finalist, Sawtooth Poetry Prize, Asahta Press, Boise State University.

Special thanks to those who have supported both me and my work along the way: Rob McLennan, Lara Candland Asplund, C.D. Wright, Arthur Sze, Phillip Morgan, Medbh McGuickian, Jeanetta Calhoun Mish, Carol Koss, Gary & Sandy Bolton, Rachel Honeywell Moran, Jim Honeywell, Elizabeth Honeywell Gray, Jimm & Jackie Jacobs, Kurt Atkinson, Doug Zook, Sherman Souther, Caleb Paull, Anselm Berrigan, Elizabeth Robinson, Yun Wang, Jonathan Stalling, Jack Jordan, Tony Navarro, Delphine Piguet, Kaci Huffman, Fr. Dwight Helt, Fr. Joe Ted Miller, Kate, Tracy, & Kade Jackson, Forrest Gander, Rilla Askew, J.I. Abbott, Thomas Jones, Lee Chapman, Jennifer Moxley, Doug Martin, Deb Klowden, Ben Lerner, Jean Valentine, Amatoritsero Ede.

A very special thank you to the beloved matriarchs who have passed this life who inspired poems and shared sacred stories: Lottie Marie, Charlotte, and Beulah Honeywell, Bessie Mae Sparks, Ruby Sparks Autrey, Orane Goode.

Contents

A Theology of Soil
A Theology of Soil	1
Closed Rooms	2
Making of real and unreal	3
Grinding into Wood	4
All directions of an open field	5

Emmenagogues and Motherhood
Ultima Thule 1945	9
Call it sky	10
By Late Morning	11
Of wash rooms	12

A Grace o' Sundays
... A Grace o'Sundays	17
II.	18
III.	19
IV.	20
V.	21
VI.	22
VII.	23

Flour Sack Appliques
Indian Head Appliqué	27
Streets as Elsewhere	28
North to their wives and dying hymns	30
The world on occasion	31
Here the world on occasion	32

Tonics Against Fevers of the Malarial Type

Ramparts of sound	35
Under pretext of music	36
Down this wall of heat	38
May without rain	39
I.	39
II.	40
Tract of level country	41
I.	41
II.	42
III.	43
Skirt Hill	44
I.	44
II.	46
III.	47

The Northernmost Habitable Region

August and Rain	53
Are there only avenues in the Holy Land?	55
I.	55
II.	56
After Birds	57
The Look of a River	58
Erasures	59
Slow after moonset	60
Small upon the Sill	61
Are we far to the forest?	63

Aubades

The arsenic furnace	67
A stream of dead water and a silk handkerchief	68
Blue Flagged	69

Do we breathe as rain?	70
(Hold these tree limbs	71
as you hold out for song)	71
Our hands tie in other ports	72
Disorders of skin	73
Certitude	74
A Note on the Cover Map and Photograph	1

Streets as Elsewhere

J.L. Jacobs

You will close your eyes.
In the eye of the crow who flies before you,
you will watch yourself
leave yourself behind.

–Paul Auster

A Theology of Soil

A Theology of Soil

For which god a certain spiral course?

I regret every distinct
object.
Think of her mouth.

Start again:	Outside my door
sideways walk.	Just one word she wanted
and rain toward summer.

The trees tell it.

Sister.	Lie down in the hollow.

Clocks lately broken and blackbirds
together are a sign.

We may listen	here
to the beginning of woods deciduous
and strange.

Lie down.   Repeat.   These her words.

Repeat.

This pasture land.
Snake country in evening.

There will be no fabulous birth stones.

I hear you	forward
over dust.

Fog slides in	settles in the road.
Hide her there
a good piece from the house.

Closed Rooms

Do not re-call me into mornings   either.
They hold us together   the zodiac
and the porch.

I unsettle your name.
Remember for an instant her under locust trees.
Her absence in the field.

Will you hear all I say?

Requiem as art.   Feed on me
that river-light.

It was strange impressions I was searching for,
a certain dryness of mouth as a sweep of wind.

This is the image of our unlit room.

Making of real and unreal

Our dreams manifest   memory
sister-girl-self   interspersed like water marks.

When she was a child it was the dream of the body
the other face   thrown into evening
moving in too small rooms.

Through rain the hawthorn and far off
footsteps.   There are deserted walls
faces behind chimneys of fever five days coming.
You sing night hymns of pure water and abolished roads.

Saint Christopher protect us in distant lands.
Already the boat   eucalyptus boiling.
Call the smell
onto a handful of leaves.

How many nights they wash the head of the corpse
with water in which basil leaves have been dropped.

Grinding into Wood

So we began.
Three days singing praises.

I inhabit this house.
Long halled
rehearsals
ceremonious beneath sycamores.

Outsized knives.   Dead ants.
Stress each syllable. Her syllables.
A third.
A fourth.
It takes concentration.

All directions of an open field

I see only two young girls
on an attic stair
to sit the night with a corpse.

Gumdrops   the dead woman   and I
with a brown paper sack.

I think in her behalf.   Stones
to the far North.
Inside this body.   Insected
language of night as we are aware.
Already the map.
And you expect her to be beautiful.

Re-arrange us in rows.
Geometric shapes   echoes of inner skin
and one   transformed.
Elsewhere of dark falling
of a girl's place in the wingspan.

Emmenagogues and Motherhood

Ultima Thule 1945

But at this time there are no remains of that nation.

What water I have here   sits stagnant.
It is your prayer and your small hands to the wrist.

We know the mountains   the seven sisters themselves
and the look of a woman through a window.

I return to the well in hopes of seeing her.
A farfetched woman   a poet   even in summer.
And still turn eyes   garb and manner.

Darkness comes down quickly
and clouds gather black to the North by noon.

It is her throat and her hands.
A borrowed woman who moves
slow-footed   backward   within her house.

A dreamer might see this:
and count the echoes—her turning shoulders
of shoes—outright. And did their eyes on trees?
Then the moon?

We sing her   of her dance over a dark girl's shoulder.

Of a storm an hour ago   and mist
that is ever-more-constant.

I know also the hymn   as rain knows night   or
an old house in a clearing   and She
choked with flowers.

Call it sky

Remember the hard earth and the ash
which spreads?   Call it sky. And so
green of summer in the name of blue
or   false indigo.

I remember words etched (into)
panes of glass in her room
of broken clocks.   A closed room.
No children   come. Or will come.

Roots in the deepest well   or
simply a flower.

(Retrace the spell of breath in a land promised
as far as into my body.)

This empty house listens to the landscape.

River noise   unnamable   and autumn.
We find here the Holy Ghost Orchid
and a bird   from distances.

Enter the skin of remoteness
as the unborn   else   a harvest.

I witness the wall   unlisting
pale yellow   inside and pass bare windows.
I long to pull open their cupboards.

What does the room?

In her sleep: the placement of the moon above the chimney.

By Late Morning

The household   or portrait
of older doorways
is in alignment with the floorboards.

With three   fingers only children
buried in the foundations of bridges.
Hymn of lost sight.

As a woman cast
new lace
for a number of babies interred
at the corners of sundry rooms.

Under giant tree roots
afternoon comes   feathers of sorrow
and
    bells in rain   again with autumn.

(At evening who will stand to watch?)

Raiment of sea as a fixed token.
(Wall of water.)

Wait against the spiked fence
or stone doorstep   by late morning.

Dust as it is seen is swept inwards
as a dream at noon.

Of wash rooms

There is an old custom of passing sickly children
nine times over and under
a blackberry stem   rooted   at both ends.

Behind the still room lay the garden.
House in whose ruins they were found.
In another a blue bird   set
in a rocky landscape.   One of the frescoes has
a blue monkey. There is vetch, day lilies
and a woman walking up the dusty road.
Straight uphill.

Wooden houses stand as near.
Bayberry and wildroses and the scattered farms.
Seaward windows in rows.

Birdskin and cobweb truth accumulate as rain on leafstalks.

To name canals here in the place of the maple forest. I watched
water moccasins   blue   April thunder.
I called the moon
of her unseen feet and the hills or stream in rains.

This is weather.   Six years into silence and prayers.
A glass face
       becoming   part of the forest.
I will dream you seaward   so far and far.

There are wild bees in a memory of old women stretching fabric.
It is a small room.   Their narrow hands
clock to wall   mark edges
with darkness below.   A hidden side-door.

To see your own gray hands wrapping . . . warping.   Light
veers under fingernails.   She sensed a direction
of washrooms   years ago.   A seven month birth
                and moonlight up the wall three nights.

*Dreams fray   near the window   the widow
near the child with the wild red hair . . .*

I don't know if this has anything to do with place   as in geography
when I look at her or the dry river-bed.   It is autumn.
A drought year.

False doorways are to be entered backwards
as taut skin from an unbecoming angle.

See the position of viewer relative to corpse   cut off thighs,
sectioned clitoris.

I am driving west on an empty road home.

I remember the story of a woman who kept in her lover's stead
a jar of sweet basil.   That is all I remember.

We enter October as cold trees.

Here is a meaning alternating blue.   Bird, spider,
the unmarried mother and so on.

A Grace o' Sundays

"O, you must wear your rue with a difference."
Hamlet IV.v

. . . A Grace o'Sundays
for Kate

I.

They are here
cruel throated reds
and rose petals sealed in a jar.

It is her own dispensary:

to sleep next a sister
to sit on her bones.

II.

Remember the baby girl with the blue blue eyes
that wouldn't close?

These are the second hand accounts of locals
in continual vibration
limb to limb   as you collect models,
FLORENTINE women,
and songs of ether.

Was it the slender neck of morning
and catfish that can be raised any-where?

III.

You know the darts.
The arrows thrown.
She stripped on a table at Clyde's Tue
and drove the Slim Road home without headlights.

This country was dark   back then.

Your blue granite.   Her guitar.   Your Indian baby.

And gray squirrel as a delicacy.

IV.

Remember her white cotton slip?

Days   down alleys
on estimates of rain.

It is to sleep standing   facing North.

Crow-songed.
Cross-sawed.

Translated as suddenness.

V.

You bear witness to the most beautiful song sung the way of evening.

To awaken the child   snake-rooted.

It is
one mad dance

      under fresh spells
and newly washed linen.

And she
naked on her knees

advances

sister-less.

VI.

I feed you bits of bread.

Hear the reply of tea
translated   (in your mouth.)

A certain black powder.
A choice remedy.

The next proposition:
Rooted oaks proceed finite
so soon as
pores of your skin.

VII.

There are beautiful abstracts
We draw   toward a name.
World their doctrine.

The clock,
as if a lover asked
of our blue dot   history.

To be heard.
To speak of bread.

So we traveled.

Flour Sack Appliques

Indian Head Appliqué

Two women dream river currents.
Curving points.

The fact of her   (held).

Cut out her name.   Hum it now.

Habit of atonement.
Their branching inlaid
as one inlaid chair   to be marked
for dying.

A circle so
full of sewn   hemmed even.
Forward in its edges
in preparation for years.   To form
a blueprint.

I put my mouth as near
and use words

                downwards.

Streets as Elsewhere

She says noise as birds.
If I of song
or wisteria,
count years on a postcard.

Which stands more solid in this cooler climate?

She had streets as elsewhere
and lived to round a chairmaker.
Houses starved of paint.
If not pale, sun-dyed
landscape
under hyacinth blue.

Today the sycamores
stood four acres in water.

She glanced up from the card table
to the door,
a face in front rooms.

She thought of sailors,
holy waters.

Recognized black gum burning
and visitors arriving too early.

Men, she said, fall over their own
shadows on summer nights.

His story in a diary,
flesh and marigolds and a light
beneath stairs.

She brought him hard bread
long after dark.
Its curfew bell reminds
a town of white stone
and someone complaining about the rains.

North to their wives and dying hymns

You will lift a curtain and I plot
the angle.   Your throat as dry.
There are names beyond us.   Beyond her
barefooted morning.

Finger her ear. Enlarged.   As under
blue. You are a sound delayed
before a rainstorm   dismantled.   She
toward a more calculated pale   childlike   hairless.
A clearer memory of wings and the sun at mid-afternoon.

This is the basin of the foothills.   Disordered wood
mild and more near. Who will plant the late lands?
I repeated.   I remained to eavesdrop as a heron
on one leg.   Ledged roots in.

The world on occasion

Thicket becomes here
the body
re-called   birdlike.

Dry weather   foregrounded.
The distance, its fields.

Or an overheard song: soon
set root against cold

and so much of water.
Entered or wished in conversation.
It cannot last.   Sing here between them.

Here the world on occasion

Believe in the Catalpa   as a sign
smell to re-call
white petals at your waist
taken completely   as evening pulled in.

Can I expect unbraiding?
Your feet as clues?

I stand more firmly this one tree
the smallest roadmap   named

empty of absolution.

My skin in evidence.

Tonics Against Fevers of the Malarial Type

Ramparts of sound

There is no further trace of the painter
and wall
this house out of heathen legend.

Her feet in our boat.
In a green meadow I saw madness.
Were singing.

There is a word which means   dark or blue
or the black stream.   Having spent years there
darkening mountains — sea-caved and frayed.
Walk before me   still   the door.

She was fond of roads in-land.

Now light into cellars   this lamp.
Clockwork of sky.

Somewhere a screen door slams.   Ramparts
of sound   crowed into afternoon
as others.

Under pretext of music

The document gave names.   Disorders.
Birth defects.   Disfigurement as ailment.

Carry me toward e-migration.
Iconoclast and my colic.

Calls to prayer.

Intervening days: climate mild and more near.
A different landscape.
Windswept   lack of wood
and detailed temperature.

At evening we collect upon pretext of music.

Suddenly,
a second child in sketched muslin.

It was a summer storm   against your
metronome.   April thunder.
A ballet piece.

North cadence I am after;
lamplight in-doors at evening.

Simple
geometry of movement   pedals
to please you.

Weather re-combining.
Cold June.   Just remaindered,
as if this were another place.

(Imagine that it is.)

In the panes   incandescence
strewn shapes   branches
in rain.

(The girl breathes deep.)

I studied dust
collection   and re-collection of dust.
And thought of trees.

Down this wall of heat

The house gathers dust and rushes.
(Unreadable.)

And the girl's body arches.   See
the unbecoming
angle.

I lie down now.

Open-mouthed-bird.
And trust they're all singing.

These
our only taboos: Her folded notion
of water and clear voice.
Her hand   unwrapped.

Climb in closer.
Without line these your limbs, gills,
wrist a small cut on a mid-season day.

May without rain

I.

These postcards of women.
They take of traveling.

Ascertain evening
six hundred miles across the Gulf
vertical green.

Recurrence of morning.
Hear
recognizable night freight.

(Strange benefit of geography.)

II.

I found your instructions   folded.

Translate encounters   magpies
in the sky   on the ground
as suddenness.

We have outmapped water.
Steady handed archer
the apple and a new way
to aim.

Dark as our night sky.

Tract of level country

I.

Shantung blue   her June of
rain.
Everywhere
vegetables and the smell of their ripeness
unbearable.

And us separate.

Malaria lowland a procession
of equinoxes.
As we saw.

(We of all observers.)

Her house
skid across the flood plain.

Her patterns   cut from the *Kansas City Star*
tulips drawn
for her sister's Indian Head appliqué.

Take her voice   from the two storey house.
See here storms   and drizzle
at the bottom of the well.

II.

Out of this what returns?

She sketches charcoal on cotton
as bone, cartilage
or hooves on marshy soil.

Mark the year and adorn
her throat.

III.

Dreams red into knives
and expected
miracles.

Two women move.

Blot out the sky
or honest days in heat.

Single voiced gin
and morning glories.

Nothing more landlocked.

Skirt Hill

I.

Tonight I want grapes.

A transfusion of birds
like fingers into hands

    slow closing

strangely frail buttonholes.

You harbour sour wine:
Full throated ghost
unworked hair   and all

the night behind.

You laid the tongue and groove
of my pine ceiling.
Your message   mortal.
Not to tell.

Go forth from here
the river road.

I inhabit your garden.

My hand mid-thigh
upwards
part-song   (echoed)

and a row of trees
ensued by mud.

Dream distance
and the no-road-back.
Listen in the thatch-eaved
kitchen.

(Storms and all that is comprehensible.)

The circumstance of my name
and yours.
Telescoped senses and closed lids.

II.

Level reach   of rain

I walk in.

I have sealed all the jars.

Moved between farm houses
copperhead wary,

as always in late autumn,

>   slow-moving
>   unfettered voice.

I sorted linens,
uncreased cotton flour sacks
with mitered corners.

We lived below Skirt Hill.

The North side of the house
unshingled.

Open to indeterminate sleep
and my inconstancy.

III.

It was a June rehearsal.
The Choctaw in cuffless
trousers   hard-dried.

And she drinking blue
like wine.

It is a prison song.

You insisted in her,
a red-brown girl   moved
(lengthwise) across the floor

swanless
                into words.

I wrist into morning
digging
        earthing in
and the house like me
tin-roofed
pelted.

I have overwatered everything
as sacrament.
        Re-collected grocery lists.
Your sense of chairs
        re-ordered.

This wall of books
that hover my skin —
such an Easter
hoping
        dark to bone.
Its colour blue in mind
as fruit.

I heard a rhythm of flowers
in our unlit room
        thickening dust
        circles of dark tobacco
at a distance.

A sun for sun   draped August
a road
upended.   Black-top ready.

Trees on the occasion

of months   fractured

Oaks, sweetgum, sycamores
          bulldozed to widen
the road North
          to lower the hill ten inches.

It is my own posture
my high-shoes.
I grow cold on the porch.

I see dirt and stillbirths
and
try   to stay awake.

The Northernmost Habitable Region

August and Rain

I am two women pressed against
one another
in this narrow bed.

Will you know me when I stand?

Smoke from burning leaves
in autumn, yet unnamed.

The lilacs past my window are gone.

I am within and no children come
or will come.

Migration of birds
flocks of white or rasp of sound.

Departures in August and rain
call me out of dreams.

I see you at night
in the corner where your hairs collect
by the closet door.

I have them. Bits of you
in vials, old shopping lists,
medicine paper clipped in a drawer.

My feet in the floorboard
on your close pulled feather pillow.

It was your smell I was after.

For years I dreamt you
a wish-making map
inside of stone.

It is early still
and it is your long back that I love,
but I know I'll pull down half
heaven when you go.

Are there only avenues in the Holy Land?

I.

Of your hair
and the angel in your eyes.
They stare out to sea.
Your throat and skin   cold, blanched.

I awaken in the dark to a quaint notion of ancient geographers
and it is from woman back to woman
with one walking beside you.
Singing.   Her name does not translate.
It is her hair and her voice falling of pastorals that range apart.

Dreams cross and dying voices rattle.
I meet with children, here. Follow rivers laid down in Dutch charts.

Who will recall sleep?
I met all the women
yet   one woman   singular
between the cradle and the bed.

It will end she says with angels
in a wine cellar.
We have faith   but the oaks are motionless.
Ancestral posturing toward this distant stronghold.

See here charts for navigating the most distant lands.

II.

We are dismantling a house
slowly   in short   her inward parts.

(Far off among the trees a night fisherman wades upstream.)
He crosses under the moon   and sees
a girl standing by a ferry rail.

Snake-doctors in the dusk.   Birds, as long faces
vision into mountains.
These are my nightmares of over-ripened fruit.   Cut open.

You are asleep. Your lost face near.
Your heart into trees. It is the same earth
houses, strange, distended and I cannot find you.

After Birds

You remember after birds
a girl's door   feather of summer

on beautiful feet.

Dry white bones keep the big hill solid
standing   looking at you
humming.

It is a different light that falls   and blonde floorboards.

Purple dye of myriad herds.

What shepherd repeats the sound?

Birds' heads scattered

abandoned.

Conjecture substitutes for the Apostle's name.

The Look of a River

Pray the moon   unbreathing.
My hand for the dark of fish.

Morning of ripened fruit
and of your sorrow.
Let lovers go fresh
wrapped in clean linen.

I remember a woman and water in my throat.

It is dead reckoning that suffers
the drift of water
and a repeat of wind.

And I in cool bedclothes
dream those were nine years
like summer
down from the hill farms and pastures.

An open window   awakened
you were a child on a white bed
so late in April.

It was a three mile wide river
and goats that still abound the *Holy Ghost*
from an overland return.

Erasures

A slow sound   I remember how
and night's opening
accumulations of an hour.

Rain dried in moonlit bushels

feminine
as if put in order by her hand
half-blue and bluer.

I had dreamt of braids   the face oval,
but this woman was large against you.
She fills the room.

I remember you told me how the insides of her thighs
lay peacefully   and your eyes turn
or will turn.

(We have kept our erasures in order, here.)
Their dooryards   hold up the river,
songs travel downstream.

But against this, tell it to me, all of it,
from the beginning into the distant seacoast
and against it.

And our bodies also in the half-light. Or
there may have been: leaves full of voices
an upturned nipple   crescent of blue-shot waters
and she toward the window.

Slow after moonset

At morning there are flowers.

She has come early.   Azalea
in a folktale.

We will preserve her eyes or through the dawn
the gray of her braids.

This woman   (large against you)
in so many dreams.

There was wild mint as you told
me how.
Beyond that, she believes not.
Which is to say: No other taste changes and trees
grow in water.   Or simply that her skirts brushed your
thighs.

Lights flicker in small jars on the front porch
and the day is between a door
and a door and black on the roof tiles.

This is the immoderate love of women.

Small upon the Sill

I wanted strewn rooms.   A delicacy of words.

Doorway to follow the road.   One by one.

My mouth is rung to determine festivals
and the silvered girl   enters
behind the mirror.

(Here she escapes.)

Tree after leaf and paradise extended.

Birds   even more
You.

(There is a flatness to what remains.)
Further heresy of dark hair.

I should say: wash in a southward stream.
Exalt yourself to frustrated rain and womanliness

(in a darkened room.)

I wanted no curtains.

Preoccupied all one midnight.

To know summer in your second-storey window
toward your pointed ceiling   upward like sparrows
in the eaves.

Rain against the sills
in liquid arrows   pierce
our many partings   sound stairwells
inhabit walls
Angel to Irving Avenue

under a sky which does not spread,
if we say we are longing.

Are we far to the forest?

Climb over me.
It is the ashes of tomorrow   (vetch of a distant past.)
It is insomnia   into the hallways of the sleeper.

Her feet alone in my fable.   She
seeking only haste.

Which is under the skin.

I come to bury
and you leave us   (one summer evening)
as an ode to a stone.

Vigil and feast of men   and toward the sea *her own story.*

The holy women in orchids.   Her women
their mouths full of black colts.

Animals at pasture turn slow eyes.

Footsteps resound.   All traces of lace which were her body
form a breast.

The woman stands on the threshold.
Her face   as salt through rain.

Imagine where landscape begins.   Beyond deserted walls
faces behind chimneys   of fever   five days coming
of pure water and abolished roads.

I preserve the smell of overcoats in rain   of women fallen
whispering the highest steeple.

AUBADES

The arsenic furnace

Questions of light
at 4 a.m.
and unchangeable heat.

Is it unleavened bread only?

Finger to hand
a promise.

I weed
the blue-tiled walkway
to stand an audible
radiant escape.

A stream of dead water and a silk handkerchief
for Caleb

Slow over stones.

To know your noise   as a moth beating a curtain.
You wrap yourself at night
until you happen to dream
of a man   with a woman's passion
who   gathers up the room   in the room —
so let them.

Between this night and morning   it was your prayer.
Or who would have found a painter this night?
Your small hands to the wrist as you stood   in the door
and stood between.

Blue Flagged

We go on weightless
bridged to and from
stories you may not remember.

And this word   (timbre)
called in as a ghost.
Stand still.
Know the names.
The sleeves of song.

(And a certain alto voice.)

Do we breathe as rain?

They found a bag of asafetida tied around her neck.
Heavy streeted
religion.

She reads of Flemish Masters   assumes
a blind canal,
and pronunciation.

Name her Saint. Vistas
and only numbered doors.

Smell of cognac and persimmons.

I send you this telegram,
this sketch of a woman
cobalt-blue.

*(Hold these tree limbs
as you hold out for song)*

Come here

      each morning.

Paint me white   (as in)   more pale.

April walking   andare.   As it is understood.
And water moccasins   (here)
in the road.

Chiaroscuro is it not?

The droughted pond.
And your own unswerving atlas.

Our hands tie in other ports

He freely translates
what he sees as her shoes.
No word for wren
or hairbreath escapes.

Of trees   turn now
ceremony of hands   or
rain that can be danced into falling.

Disorders of skin

Rain   (as it will). And
it is dusk.
And you with song upon slim voice.

There is need:
A reminiscence.   (Partaken.)
Baptized Presbyterian.

We remember the names.
The names.   Their passing.
Were days
or something close.   Closed.
Coiled in our attic bed.
To wrap ourselves (us even)
as it would be.

(There was singing   a cappella.)

Underneath   I
pulled into your own bones.

Certitude

(July evenings occur as a name repeated.)

Strange benefit of geography.

He studied me at mirrors
but recalled   only photographs
and houses leaning   seasonal
(a deluded shoreline.)

Ascertain bird   or cicada   near.
Awaken to a darkened background
clouded North by noon.

Here is a reverse.   We take of gales
and a landscape of driving rain.

It is the tangled white hair
of two decades
(definition.)

It is the perfect blur of reflection.

A Note on the Cover Map and Photograph

Ancient maps stir the coals of our hearts' memories, letting us see from whence we came. Maps often remember what the mind forgets, like home-made bridges, foot-logs, and corduroy roads. Maps don't remember the trials and travails, letting us forget the bumps and stumps in the road, delivering us to our new homes in the Territory. To remember that just a few miles to the east edge of this map is the place called Ultima-Thule, called so by Missionaries who accompanied the Choctaws' from Mississippi on that dreaded Trail of Tears to their new home-the edge of the known world—"the northernmost habitable region."

This map represents the southern and easternmost corners of Indian Territory, once part of Arkansas, and now Oklahoma. There is one road in, one road out into Arkansas, with the other two exits being the Albion ferry, DeKalb ferry and the Clarksville ferry. Hi-way 70 was gravel til 1948. Streets here like no-where else.

This map is also the terrain of the 'Midwife' of Stevens Creek valley and Little River Basin who had to walk mile after mile, as work came by a rider and his horse.

Standing here, your Grandmother Charlotte is photographed by your Great-Grandmother Lottie Marie, the Midwife. Charlotte's father milled the trees out of these hills before anyone had a conscience about it. They did save the best white pine timbers for coffins; your Grandmother lined those coffins & closed the eyes of the dead. She birthed babies, too, and sat with the sick.

Her calling didn't allow for sorrow or lament, and the gifting of the called propelled her, as God never repents of his calling on a person's life of service. Her unfailing service granted her life into the 21st century, from a wagon train to manned shuttles to the moon.

She was gifted a lucid one hundred years of life.

~Jimm Jacobs

Photo by Melanie Jennings

JL Jacobs grew up in Oklahoma underfoot to her great-grandmother who was midwife and root-doctor to a small community at the end of the Trail of Tears (forced removal of Choctaws to Indian Territory 1830-32). She studied art, photography and literature, and graduated from Brown University's MFA Program. Her work has appeared in such journals as *Ploughshares*, *New American Writing*, *New Orleans Review*, *American Letters & Commentary*, *Volt*, *Five Fingers Review*. Books include, *Varieties of Inflorescence*, Leave, 1992, *The Leaves in Her Shoes*, Lost Roads, 1999, and *DreamSongs*, Above Ground Press, 2004. Recent work has appeared in *Fascicle*, *Octopus*, *American Letters & Commentary* and *Ploughshares*. She lives and writes in the Cross Timbers of America—where the eastern woodlands meet the Great Plains.